P9-CQN-068

Hillary Clinton

by Jodie Shepherd

Content Consultant

Nanci R. Vargus, Ed.D.
Professor Emeritus, University of Indianapolis

Reading Consultant

Jeanne M. Clidas, Ph.D.
Reading Specialist

Children's Press®
An Imprint of Scholastic Inc.
New York Toronto London Auckland Sydney
Mexico City New Delhi Hong Kong
Danbury, Connecticut

Library of Congress Cataloging-in-Publication Data
Jodie Shepherd.
  Hillary Clinton/by Jodie Shepherd; poem by Jodie Shepherd.
    pages cm. — (Rookie biographies)
  Includes bibliographical references index.
  Audience: Ages 3-6.
  ISBN 978-0-531-20592-1 (library binding: alk. paper)— ISBN 978-0-531-20994-3
(pbk.: alk. paper)
1. Clinton, Hillary Rodham—Juvenile literature. 2. Presidents' spouses—United States—
Biography—Juvenile literature. 3. Women legislators—United States—Biography—
Juvenile literature. 4. United States. Congress. Senate—Biography—Juvenile
literature. 5. Women politicians—United States—Biography—Juvenile literature. 6.
Women presidential candidates—United States—Biography—Juvenile literature. 7.
Women cabinet officers—United States—Biography—Juvenile literature. I. Title.

  E887.C55S475 2015
  327.730092—dc23 [B]   2014035679

No part of this publication may be reproduced in whole or in part, or stored
in a retrieval system, or transmitted in any form or by any means, electronic,
mechanical, photocopying, recording, or otherwise, without written permission
of the publisher. For information regarding permission, write to Scholastic Inc.,
Attention: Permissions Department, 557 Broadway, New York, NY 10012.

Produced by Spooky Cheetah Press
Design by Keith Plechaty

© 2015 by Scholastic Inc.

All rights reserved. Published in 2015 by Children's Press, an imprint of Scholastic Inc.

Printed in China 62

SCHOLASTIC, CHILDREN'S PRESS, ROOKIE BIOGRAPHIES®, and associated logos
are trademarks and/or registered trademarks of Scholastic Inc.

1 2 3 4 5 6 7 8 9 10 R 24 23 22 21 20 19 18 17 16 15

Photographs ©: AP Images: cover (Achmad Ibrahim), 27, 31 center top (Carolyn
Kaster), 28 (Ed Andrieski), 31 center bottom (Kathy Willens), 8, 30 top right (Paul
Sancya); Getty Images: 3 top right (Chris Hondros), 12, 31 top (Djamilla Rosa
Cochran), 11 (Lee Balterman), 19 (Luke Frazza), 4, 30 top left (New York Daily News),
20 (Pornchai Kittiwongsakul), 16 (Ramin Talaie); Reuters: 23, 24; Thinkstock: 3 top left
(Dan Thornberg), 31 bottom (Digital Vision); U.S. State Department: 3 bottom; William
J. Clinton Presidential Library: 15.

Table of Contents

Meet Hillary Clinton

Hillary Clinton has been the first lady of the United States, a United States **senator**, and the **secretary of state**. She has fought to help people around the world. She is an inspiration to people everywhere.

Clinton marches with Girl Scouts in a Memorial Day parade.

Hillary Rodham was born in Chicago, Illinois, on October 26, 1947. She loved playing outside with her two younger brothers, Hugh and Tony. Hillary also loved school. She was a very good student.

MAP KEY

Illinois

● City where
Hillary Clinton
was born

Wisconsin

Michigan

Lake
Michigan

Iowa

Chicago ●

Illinois

Indiana

Missouri

Kentucky

Arkansas

Tennessee

This photo of Clinton and her mom was taken at a political event in 2007.

As Clinton grew up, she saw that many children did not have as much as she did. Some were poor. Some lived in neighborhoods that were not safe. Clinton's mother taught her to always help others.

FAST FACT!

Clinton thought about being an astronaut. But when she wrote to the astronaut program at age 14, she was told: No girls allowed.

After high school, Clinton went to Wellesley College in Massachusetts. She liked being at a school that was just for women. No one told her she could not do the things she wanted to do.

This is a photo of Clinton from when she was in college.

After college, Clinton went to Yale Law School. There she became even more interested in the problems of children and the poor.

After becoming a **lawyer**, Clinton joined the Children's Defense Fund. Her job was to make sure every child in the United States had the chance to go to school.

Clinton poses with kids from the YMCA in Harlem, New York.

Making a Home in Arkansas

About a year later, Hillary moved to Arkansas and began teaching law. She married Bill Clinton in October 1975.

In 1978, Bill was elected governor of Arkansas. As first lady, Hillary worked to improve the Arkansas schools. She also made sure that people in poor areas could get good care from doctors and hospitals.

In 1980, Hillary gave birth to her daughter, Chelsea.

This photo of Clinton and Chelsea was taken at a meeting in New York City in 2013.

Working for Others

In 1993, Bill Clinton was sworn in as president of the United States. Hillary became the new first lady.

FAST FACT!

During her time as first lady, Clinton wrote a book called *It Takes a Village*. She wrote that parents, teachers, and communities all had to be involved to help children succeed.

The Clintons wave to supporters on election night.

As first lady, Clinton worked to make sure everyone in the country could get the care they needed from doctors. She also spoke out for women and children all around the world.

Clinton is visiting kids in Thailand whose homes were destroyed by a flood.

In 2000, the Clintons moved to New York. That same year, Hillary ran to become a senator from the state of New York and won. She took office in January 2001.

FAST FACT!

Clinton is the first first lady to win elected office. She is also the first female senator from New York.

Clinton was a popular senator. She worked to make sure **veterans** and their families were well taken care of. She ran for the Senate a second time and won.

Clinton reads to children at a bookstore.

New Challenges

In 2008, President Barack Obama chose Clinton to be secretary of state. For four years, she traveled to 112 countries around the world. She worked to create good relationships between the United States and other countries.

Obama and Clinton tour Thailand together.

27

Timeline of Hillary Clinton's Life

1975
marries William Jefferson Clinton

1947
born on October 26

1980
daughter, Chelsea, is born

Hillary Clinton has always spoken out for freedom. She has stood up for the rights of women, children, and others who needed help.

What will she do next? Whatever it is, Clinton is sure to keep working to make the world a better place.

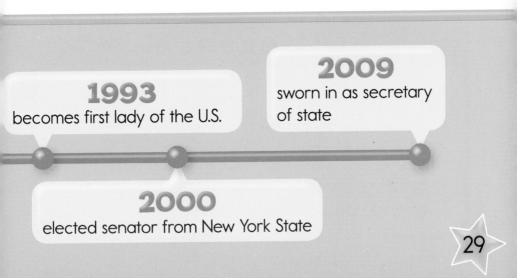

1993
becomes first lady of the U.S.

2009
sworn in as secretary of state

2000
elected senator from New York State

A Poem About
Hillary Clinton

First lady, senator, secretary of state,

lawyer and author and president's mate.

All over the world, she has won many friends;

the ways that she's helped other people never ends.

You Can Make a Difference

- Learn as much as you can about a problem.

- Before you do anything or make any decisions, listen to what others have to say.

- Speak up for what you believe in. Do not be afraid to be a leader.

Glossary

lawyer (LAW-yer): someone who is trained to advise people about the law and who speaks for them in court

secretary of state (SEH-krah-ter-ree OF STAYT): person chosen by the president to represent the United States and work with other countries

senator (SEN-uh-tor): member of a group of people who make laws for a state or country

veterans (VET-er-rans): people who have served in the military or fought in a war

Index

Facts for Now

Visit this Scholastic Web site for more information on Hillary Clinton:
www.factsfornow.scholastic.com
Enter the keywords **Hillary Clinton**

About the Author

Jodie Shepherd, who also writes under the name Leslie Kimmelman, is an award-winning author of dozens of books for children, both fiction and nonfiction. She is a children's book editor, too.

J B CLINTON

Shepherd, Jodie.
Hillary Clinton

SOF

R4002327791

SOUTH FULTON BRANCH
Atlanta-Fulton Public Library